What are others saying about this book?

Employees and team members have come to realize that there are many rewards that far transcend money. Kevin Aguanno presents a treasury of these rewards in his astute and fun-to-read '101 Ways to Reward Team Members for $20 (or Less!).'

These days, savvy businesses are thinking outside the you-know-what, and because this book's soul and spirit exists outside the you-know-what, it is what businesses are thinking as well as what they are needing.

I know a thing or two about marketing, and I know that Kevin Aguanno has made a remarkable contribution to the body of marketing wisdom with this enlightening and practical book. The only people who will enjoy it more than you will be your employees.

Jay Conrad Levinson, The Father of Guerrilla Marketing, Founder of The Guerrilla Marketing Association, Author of the Guerrilla Marketing series of books (Over 14 million sold in 39 languages)

Kevin Aguanno has assembled an inspiring collection of non-monetary rewards - none cost more than $20. Dip into his short book to find the reward that will work for you. Kevin also provides useful guidelines about finding the right reward, figuring out the right way to present the award, and determining the right reasons to give the reward.

Money is not always the best reward. Often, a reward for less than $20 can be a far more effective way to recognize contribution. The right token is eloquent in expressing praise and recognizing effort. Kevin helps readers figure out how to use thought, not cash, to praise. You can do good without spending a bundle. Kevin shows you how.

Dr. Bob Fabian, The Concept Monger, www.fabian.ca

In today's society of over loaded email inboxes, conference calls and net meetings, often times we forget to say thanks and acknowledge the contributions of those that make our projects, departments and organizations successful. Kevin's book provides a step-by-step approach to decisions regarding what type of reward to bestow and the ramifications (positive and negative) contained therein. His ideas for acknowledgement are realistic and credible and are mindful of monetary constraints. I strongly recommend this easy read to those interested in boosting company morale through the implementation of a rewards program.

Lisa Kruszewski, Project Management Institute

This is the quintessential guide book to the effective practice of rewards and recognition programs. This compilation of do's, don'ts and incentives literally cooks with appropriate, timely and cost efficient ways to motivate people. If you are a senior manager, mid-manager or a small business person overseeing a tiny team, you will benefit from deploying these profit-building designs. More importantly, you will be going one further than your competition by keeping your most valued employees satisfied.

In a business world increasingly focused on customers, your company will be able to maintain and motivate your irreplaceable assets – the employees who serve your valuable customers.

This guidebook is definitely one to keep on the bookshelf to thumb through frequently. Keeping your internal people happy so that they in turn delight your external customers is the name of the game in the future of business.

Laura Pollard, President, Customer Relationship Management Association of Canada, www.crmacanada.com

101 Ways to Reward Team Members for $20 (or Less!)

Kevin Aguanno, PMP®, MAPM

"Donisque coacti."

First Edition

Multi-Media Publications Inc. ❖ Lakefield, Ontario

101 Ways to Reward Team Members for $20 (or Less!)

by Kevin Aguanno

Published by:
Multi-Media Publications Inc.
R.R. #4B, Lakefield, Ontario, Canada, K0L 2H0

http://www.mmpubs.com/

ISBN (paperback edition):   1-895186-04-8
ISBN (PDF edition):   1-895186-09-9

First printing 2004.
Printed in Canada. Published in Canada.

National Library of Canada Cataloguing in Publication

Aguanno, Kevin, 1967-
101 ways to reward team members for $20 (or less) / Kevin Aguanno.

(The project management essentials library)
Issued also in electronic format.
Includes bibliographical references.
ISBN 1-895186-04-8

1. Incentive awards. 2. Incentives in industry. 3. Employee motivation.
4. Teams in the workplace. I. Title. II. Title: One hundred one ways to reward team members for $20 (or less) III. Series: Project management essentials library.

HF5549.5.I5A38 2004   658.3'142   C2004-900070-5

Table of Contents

Acknowledgments

I would like to thank all of those people who answered my requests for inexpensive reward ideas posted via Internet discussion groups and mass-distributed emails. Using these means, I sent out an electronic survey to over 60,000 managers and the overall response was good. It was very clear to me from the beginning that there was a great interest in this topic and the range of ideas sent to me shows that we can be very creative in overcoming financial restrictions. To name all of the contributors would be too difficult, and there would be a danger of missing someone. I would also like to extend my gratitude to the many others who have helped me by listening to my ideas and providing feedback. Since nearly every idea was suggested by more than one person, I cannot attribute specific contributions to individuals. Instead, I would like to thank everyone who contributed ideas implicitly – you know who you are.

Some of the ideas in chapters one to three evolved from an article I published in *Inside Project Management*, an element-k journal. I would like to thank Craig Watkins, managing editor, for challenging me; he forced me to revisit my thinking on the matter of what makes a good reward process, and this book benefits as a result.

While many individuals provided ideas that contribute to this work, any failings that can be found within its pages are wholly my own. If you have suggestions for improving this

book, please feel free to contact me via email at
aguanno@sympatico.ca so that they may be incorporated into a
future edition.

Dedication

To Alba, Michelina Rosa, and Sebastian Joseph with thanks for allowing me to invest some of our precious family time in this book. I love you all.

PART ONE

The Pros and Cons of Rewarding

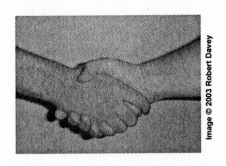

Image © 2003 Robert Davey

CHAPTER ONE

Why reward?

Everyone likes to receive praise and recognition for their good work. It starts when we are children, seeking our parents' praise and approval, and continues throughout our personal and work lives.

What do the reward recipients get from it? Different people value different aspects of rewards, but some common benefits recognized by recipients include

- Recognition of unusual efforts,

- Recognition of changed behaviours,

- Recognition of unusual accomplishments,

- Acceptance by the broader group,

- A sense of job security,

- A feeling of personal accomplishment, and

- A feeling of satisfaction.

Notice the first three points. Rewards show that the giver recognizes and appreciates that the recipient has worked harder, changed for the better, and accomplished something out of the ordinary. These are behaviours that we, as managers, want to reinforce in the recipient, as they lead to him or her being a better employee. Giving a reward for these behaviours encourages the recipient to continue h to carry on with the changes and persevere.

Rewarding someone for their positive behaviours (also called *positive reinforcement*) also has a very beneficial side effect: others on the team will see that a co-worker was rewarded for specific behaviours and will want to imitate those behaviours to receive rewards as well. Many times these indirect benefits are reason enough on their own to justify a full reward programme within an organization.

We shouldn't just reward the unusual achievements and behaviours, however. Rewarding only those at the high end of the performance curve may send a negative message to the majority of the workers who are the doing the main work of any organization. If the average worker is working hard on a daily basis, but only those with unusual accomplishments are

Employee Job Performance Analysis in a Sample Organization

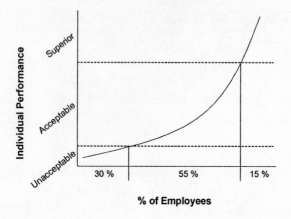

14

rewarded, the average worker may feel that there is no way he or she can ever meet those higher levels of performance. If the average worker feels that those high performance levels are unattainable, or only attainable through a lucky break, then the indirect benefits of the rewards are lost. We must notice the positive achievements of these average workers as well, and provide suitable rewards to encourage them to continue their daily drive to move the organization forward.

> *I guess the biggest comment I wanted to make is people need to be recognized a lot more than they are at the present time. [We are] great for rewarding the [high achievers] but there are a lot of regular folk whose day-to-day contributions come and go and they are never actually singled out, thanked, and given a token to make them feel like someone noticed.*
>
> Judy Conn, Project Control Officer, personal communications with the author, 2002.

Many people are strongly motivated by knowing what concrete (tangible) rewards are available to them for good performance. These people will focus on the reward, and push themselves towards great achievements. Some are motivated by money, but many are motivated by just knowing that there is a desirable, tangible reward waiting for them if they excel.

15

Rewards that have a humorous aspect create an additional benefit for the workforce – they reduce job-related stress. A good laugh from time to time releases tension, reduces blood pressure, and can improve employee job satisfaction.

Both humorous and serious rewards directly contribute to positive employee morale. With positive morale, more time is spent on productive activities and less time is spent complaining. Improved morale leads to lower employee turnover and this directly contributes to an improved bottom line.

So, rewards motivate recipients and their co-workers to improve their performance, or maintain the levels of performance at which they are already working. Rewards highlight positive behaviours and encourage recipients to continue demonstrating those behaviours. Rewards also encourage others to mimic the positive behaviours of recipients.

With positive behaviours being reinforced, employee morale will improve, and organizational effectiveness will improve, resulting in economic benefits. Reward programmes can positively impact the bottom line, improving profitability. Clearly, there is a financial case for supporting reward programmes within organizations.

A gift is as a precious stone in the eyes of him that hath it.
The Holy Bible, *Proverbs 17:8.*

Men are slower to recognise blessings than misfortunes.
Titus Livius (Livy), Roman historian. Histories, XXX, 21.

CHAPTER TWO

Rewarding is Controversial

While we all like to be appropriately rewarded, not everyone agrees that reward programmes are always in the best interests of an organization. Some people have objections to giving out rewards at all, in any situation. Others agree that, while there are situations when rewarding is appropriate, issues arise over the size of prospective rewards.

The controversy over rewards has arisen largely due to examples of the misuse of rewards in the past. Managers have used rewards to manipulate team members in inappropriate ways, often leading to bitterness among team members. Sometimes, a team member may feel unfairly ignored if a reward programme is seen as "playing favourites." Giving out inappropriate rewards may offend or anger recipients. And even if you get all of these things right, you may give out rewards too freely, devaluing the rewards, and reducing the ability of the reward programme to motivate team members to change (or reinforce) behaviours.

Rewarding at All

Let's first look at the controversy over whether we should reward at all. Some critics of reward programmes do not like the fact that rewards highlight superior performance. By its very nature, giving out a reward distinguishes between individuals and praises one over another. To some people, this differentiation is unfair, and leads to fears of favouritism, manipulation, and inequality.

Since rewards are given out based upon someone's performance, such schemes by their very nature indicate that you are evaluating individual performance levels within the organization. In unionized environments, this is often a contentious issue. Many unions want their members to be seen as all the same in capability and performance, thus better protecting the jobs of those who may be performing under their capability, or under the norm for their group. Simply admitting that performance is being tracked on an individual level may lead to strike action and heated conflict in organizations with strong unions.

> *High achievers love to be measured, when you come down to it, because otherwise they can't prove to themselves that they are achieving.*
>
> Dr. Robert Noyce, cofounder of Intel Corporation, quoted in *1001 Ways to Reward Employees* by Bob Nelson.

While those earning praise like to have their accomplishments measured and recognized, there is a danger in praising individuals: if you praise one person for his or her performance, you are not praising others for their own performance, and feelings may be hurt. You might formally recognize the special contributions of one team member, but not notice that someone else worked just as hard behind the scenes. If you praise the first, the second could feel left out and that his or her work is not valued. Another time, you might formally reward someone, but not realize that the recipient was just the spokesperson for a whole group of people. While some rewards might be shared within the contributing team, others, such as a free massage at a nearby spa, cannot be shared among individuals. In such cases, the spokesperson could not share the reward with his or her teammates even if he or she wanted to do so. You can easily create feelings of jealousy, resentment, and unhealthy competition that can rip apart a well-functioning team. You need to be careful when rewarding to avoid this.

Why give out rewards at all? Some people believe that rewards are not necessary. After all, we are all adults, and know whether we have done good work or not. These same people believe that, if we happen to recognize superior performance anyway, we should limit ourselves to verbal praise. As adults, we should see the "thank you" of our superiors as reward enough for a job well done: we

---

The reward of a thing well done is to have done it.

Ralph Waldo Emerson, American author, poet, and philosopher, *Essays. First Series. New England Reformers*

should already feel rewarded through our sense of accomplishment and recognition that we have done our best. Adding the praise of our superiors is simply "icing on the cake" – not necessary, but welcomed.

When responsible action, the natural love of learning, and the desire to do good work are already part of who we are, then the tacit assumption to the contrary can be fairly described as dehumanizing.

Alfie Kohn, American author and lecturer, *Punished by Rewards*, 1999.

The only reward of virtue is virtue.

Ralph Waldo Emerson, American author, poet, and philosopher, *Essays. First Series. Friendship.*

Diamond me no diamonds! Prize me no prizes!

Alfred Tennyson, British poet, *Idylls of the King. Elaine.*

To set the cause above renown, To love the game above the prize.

Sir Henry John Newbolt, British poet and historian, *The Island Race. Clifton Chapel*

Size of Rewards

There is also some controversy over the size of rewards. Some people become concerned that rewards could be too small or too large, and cause problems either way. Let us examine those two cases.

Rewards that are Too Small

A small reward could be seen as an insult to someone working unusually hard to achieve a superior performance. Such an individual may feel that he or she has made significant personal sacrifices. Giving someone with these feelings a reward that he or she perceives as being too small could cause insult.

Let's look at Tina (not her real name). Tina is a sales representative for a local cleaning supplies company. Tina had a sales target of $2 Million in 2002. She worked extremely hard all year trying to make that target. She made dozens of phone calls every day to current and potential customers trying to drum up additional sales. She visited all one hundred of her largest customers in person, asking for their business. She prepared sales account plans and customer presentations in the evenings and on weekends. She even postponed her summer vacation so that she could work on winning the cleaning supplies contract for the local school board before the start of the school year in September. In all, she made tremendous personal sacrifices and worked harder than she had before in her entire career.

In the end, she made her sales target, but only by a slim margin. Only one other sales representative was able make his target that year.

21

When the time came for the office Christmas party in mid-Decmeber, the time bonus cheques were traditionally distributed, Tina anticipated a big bonus. She went out and bought a new outfit to attend the party – after all, she might have to get up in front of the whole company and accept an award and make a speech, like she saw someone do two years earlier, when she first started with the company.

Bonus envelopes were distributed to the employees when they arrived at the party. Tina didn't open hers right away, but waited to see the reactions of her peers. Most seemed to be thankful for the bonuses they received, even surprised to get one at all, given the tough economic climate.

Tina slowly opened her envelope, waiting to count the zeros in her bonus cheque. She only got to two. Her bonus cheque was $400. Tina was shocked. She expected at least $5,000 plus some type of formal award, perhaps a plaque. None was given. She showed it to her co-workers thinking that a mistake was made. Perhaps they missed a zero at the end of the amount...

This project was my baby for over a year. After all the hours I invested, management had the nerve to pat me on the back and give me a cheap gold pen. How patronizing! I have news for them – I didn't do all that hard work for empty praise or a cheap prize. I did it because I'm the best person for the job. I wanted to see it happen and it did. This makes it feel like my accomplishments are ordinary. I didn't just fix the fax machine or something.

[Anonymous] Quoted in an article by Jody Urquhart, author and speaker, 2002.

What was going through Tina's mind? She felt that her sacrifices and contributions were not valued highly enough. She felt taken advantage of, and was very discouraged.

Her co-workers, who also thought that her reward was too small, were not motivated to mimic the positive behaviours and personal sacrifices that led to Tina's success. In this case, the company lost the indirect benefits of granting the reward.

The following year, sales volumes declined, despite an improving economy. What was the real reason? The sales employee morale was down and no one wanted to work very hard towards meeting his or her sales targets.

When you give out rewards, remember what I call the $POVM rule: those who got ONE dollar less than someone else are likely to be "pissed off" by the fact that they got a dollar less, and those who got one dollar more are likely to be annoyed by the fact that they ONLY got one dollar more! It's how that that MARGINAL dollar is perceived that makes the difference. So [. . .] forget trying to make small dollar differences in rewards ...say "Thanks" and get on with life!

Jeffrey Gandz, Professor and Managing Director, Richard Ivey School of Business, The University of Western Ontario, personal communications with the author, 2004.

Rewards that are Too Large

Rewards that are seen as being too large can also cause conflicts within a team. It is obvious that rewards seen by other team members as being disproportionate could breed jealousy and give the appearance of favouritism. What is often surprising, however, is that such rewards may also have a negative impact on the performance of the recipient.

Let's look at a real-world example. Mike (not his real name) is a computer programmer for a large software company. Mike's department is working on the development of the next release of a popular word processing package. Mike's own responsibility is to improve the speed of printing documents from the software package by at least ten percent.

With little effort, Mike was able, in fact, to improve the speed by fifteen percent, exceeding his target by 50 percent, though in reality he only made a marginal improvement not noticeable to most users of the word processor. Mike's supervisor gave him a reward of $2,000 for exceeding his target.

While Mike was initially surprised at receiving such a large reward for such a marginal improvement, after time he began to feel that he deserved such a large reward. What happened was that Mike got used to thinking about his performance as earning the reward. After all, how could he not deserve such a reward if he had already, in fact, earned it?

Mike's team members were shocked at the magnitude of the reward. There were others on the team who made significant improvements to the word processor that would dramatically improve the experience of those using the software; however, since they did not exceed their targets, they received no reward. Jealousy and feelings of favouritism and unfairness spread through the team. People no longer stopped by to chat with Mike, and overall team morale diminished.

The impact did not stop there, however. Mike's own performance suffered over time. After the release of this new version of the word processor software, the team was asked to work on a special project for the company president. The company needed to add the ability to sell its products from its Internet Web site. The new Web site needed to be secure, accept all major credit cards, and provide a simple means for customers to place orders.

Mike and his team jumped at the chance to work on such an important and high-profile project. Mike was given the responsibility to write the software that ensured all of the transactions were carried out in a secure fashion, safe from computer hackers.

After months of heroic efforts, the team completed the new Web site, the team rejoiced. Not only did they complete the project on time and within budget, but the Web site was independently tested by a team of computer hackers who could not crack the codes and get access to customer data – the system was secure!

When bonus time came around, the team lead got a small bonus for keeping the project under control and completing the project on time, but no one else on the team received a bonus. For most of the team members the lack of a bonus was not a problem. Mike, however, was incensed.

"Last time, I hardly had to work at all, and made only a small difference, but received $2,000," Mike said. "This time, however, I worked harder than I've ever worked before – staying up all night, working weekends sometimes – and I get nothing!"

Mike was discouraged, angered, and soon quit the company to go work for another firm. What happened? While he was initially surprised at his reward on the first project, over time he felt that he earned it. Then, when he worked much harder on the second project, and produced successful results, he felt entitled to a much larger reward. Instead, when he received nothing, he felt hurt and angered.

> *The first gift is to be regarded with affection; the second gift is taken for granted.*
>
> Chinese proverb.

Rewards must not be seen, by either the recipient or the rest of the team, as being too small or too large. Disproportionate rewards can cause problems. This is one reason why many people are uncomfortable implementing a rewards programme within their organization. They don't know how to tell what size of reward is most appropriate in a given situation. We will address this issue in Chapter 3 when we discuss how to choose appropriate rewards.

Misuse of Rewards

Other than rewards being too small or too large, there are two other potential misuses of rewards that can eliminate their benefits. Rewards cannot be seen as being too easy to earn. Also, rewards must be appropriate for the recipient. Let's look at each of those in turn.

Rewards Given Too Freely

When rewards are perceived as being given too freely, then they are devalued in the eyes of the recipients and their team members. Who gets excited about receiving a reward when everyone does, all the time? It will no longer be seen as a reward for unusual behaviour, but rather as a benefit available to all employees.

Rewards have to be varied from time to time to have any special appeal. If anyone who has perfect attendance in a given year gets a small plaque, then after a while, the award does not seem special any longer. Anyone can get one. Over the years, some employees may earn several, with each successive reward appearing less and less special in the eyes of the recipient. Instead, try to vary the reward: one year a plaque, the next year dinner at a local restaurant, and maybe a bottle of wine the following year. Varying the reward over time means that it will still feel special to the recipients, as they may have not received the specific reward item before.

Bob Nelson, the worldwide expert on implementing reward programmes in companies, and best-selling author of *1001 Ways to Reward Employees* and *The 1001 Rewards & Recognition Fieldbook*, provides a rule of thumb:

For every four informal rewards (e.g., a
thank-you), there should be a more formal
acknowledgment (e.g., a day off from
work), and for every four of those, there
should be a still more formal reward (e.g.,
a plaque or formal praise at a company
meeting), leading ultimately to such
rewards as raises, promotions and special
assignments.[1]

Inappropriate rewards

One of the most damaging risks from giving
rewards is when you select an inappropriate reward for the
recipient. Chapter 3 gives us four guidelines for selecting
and giving appropriate rewards, but what happens when
we give one that is not suitable to the recipient?

Maria (not her real name) was working as a
consultant with a large financial services firm. The
company was trying to work with Russian exporters in
developing an export financing programme to help them
in a struggling economy. After successfully completing
her work and launching the new programme, her Russian
hosts gave her a fur hat made from the finest Russian
sable as a thank-you gift for her unrelenting efforts to get
the final government backing for the programme. These
hats are highly-prized in Russia, and also in New York
where Maria lives. What possibly could be inappropriate
with this gift? Maria is a vocal animal-rights activist, and
a member of PETA (People for the Ethical Treatment of
Animals). Not only did she have no desire for the gift,

---

[1] *Nelson, Bob.* 1001 Ways to Reward Employees. *Page xvi.*

but she was also very much angered by the gift.

> *It's how you say it more than what you say!*
> Michelle Lee, Quality Assurance Reviewer, personal communications with the author, 2002.

Or consider this all-time classic blunder – giving a bottle of champagne or other wine as an award to a recovering alcoholic. This not only shows that the giver does not know anything about the recipient, but it also hurts the recipient by tempting him or her to drink again.

Not taking the time to find out about someone's likes and dislikes before buying him or her a personal gift can be insulting. The recipient may feel that you don't really care enough to get an appropriate gift, or that you don't really care about him or her as an individual.

> *The best recognition is given by individuals who consider rewards to be a win/win prospect – where both the giver and the receiver gain as a result of the process. Without this mind-set, recognition giving will probably be less than successful. The giver will be frustrated, because she thought she was doing the right thing, and the receiver will be dissatisfied because of the nonverbal messages encountered during the giving process.*
> Joan Klubnik, author of *Rewarding and Recognizing Employees*, 1995

The real reason we reward someone is that we want to encourage them to keep up the good work. If the reward is not valued by the recipient, then how motivating can the reward be? We may be wasting our time and money by giving these inappropriate rewards.

Gifts don't have to be expensive to be valued. Part Two of this book lists 101 inexpensive ideas that could make a suitable award, if you take the time to determine if it is appropriate for the recipient. Chapter 3 presents guidelines that will help you choose appropriately.

For blessings ever wait on virtuous deeds, And though a late, a sure reward succeeds.

William Congreve, British playwright, *The Mourning Bride. Act 5. Sc. 12.*

It is not strength, but art, obtains the prize, And to be swift is less than to be wise. 'T is more by art than force of num'rous strokes.

Alexander Pope, British poet and essayist, *The Iliad of Homer. Book xxiii. Line 383.*

No matter what one says, you can recognize only those matters that are equal to you. Only rulers who possess extraordinary abilities will recognize and esteem properly extraordinary abilities in their subjects and servants.

Johann Wolfgang Von Goethe, German poet,Conversations with Eckermann (March 11, 1828).

CHAPTER THREE

Guidelines for a Successful Award

U p to now, we've looked at the reasons that people reward others, and the concerns that some people have over inappropriate rewards that can cause more harm than good. So, we now see the need for rewards, and we see the things to avoid doing. What are the things that we can do to ensure our rewards are as successful as possible, giving us the maximum direct and indirect benefits?

It is important, at this point, to make a distinction between rewards and recognition. Recognition is showing others that you value their performance through various means. This could be by saying "Thank you" at the next departmental meeting, presenting a certificate of appreciation, or by simply giving a pat on the back in the hallway. Recognition also includes the giving of tokens that signify the recognition and appreciation; we call these tokens *rewards*.

Recognition as a whole, when done properly, is a congruent activity: one that is unified in its message and how the message is delivered. Insincere recognition can easily be spotted by its lack of congruence; for example, a manager could give an employee a verbal "thank you for the great job," but her body language could show that she is not entirely impressed with the performance. Cynical or sarcastic tones of voice or expressions will undermine any attempt at recognition.

Recognition only works if the giver completely agrees with the process, the value of rewarding this particular recipient, the appropriateness of the method of recognition, and is comfortable giving recognition. The non-verbal messages that make up the bulk of our communications can easily overwhelm any verbal messages we are trying co communicate.

To give recognition successfully, one must...

1. Agree with the recognition process

2. Agree that the recipient's positive behaviours or accomplishments deserve recognition

3. Agree with the method of recognition

4. Be comfortable giving the recognition.

To maximize the benefits of giving recognition (or a reward), you must believe in the reward and in the recipient. But what can we do to make sure we are giving the right reward?

Next, we will discuss four tips to choosing the right reward. Following the four tips makes sure that you have chosen a reward that will be valued by the recipient, and that is suitable for the accomplishment of the recipient. Also, when giving the reward, the tips will tell you how to make sure that the reward is seen as recognizing the right behaviours to ensure that you get the most direct and indirect benefits from the reward.

34

Four Tips to Choosing the Right Reward

1. Choose a reward that suits the person
2. Choose a reward that suits the accomplishment
3. Tie the reward to the accomplishment
4. Give the reward in a timely fashion

Choose a reward that suits the person

The first consideration that you should make when choosing a reward is the interests of the recipient. Try to choose a reward that is suited to his or her interests and beliefs. There is no point in giving an inappropriate reward that will not be appreciated or used.

When deciding upon the suitability of a reward, you must take into account the interests, beliefs, and standards of the community, the organization, the person giving the reward, and the recipient. Where there is conflict between these, find a solution that will fit the standards of all parties, else you will fail to achieve all of the benefits from the reward. The figure below shows the nested layers of interests, beliefs, and standards that you need to consider to help make your reward a success.

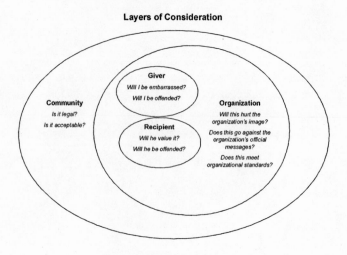

Layers of Consideration

Giver
Will I be embarrassed?
Will I be offended?

Community
Is it legal?
Is it acceptable?

Organization
Will this hurt the organization's image?
Does this go against the organization's official messages?
Does this meet organizational standards?

Recipient
Will he value it?
Will he be offended?

Community Beliefs/Standards

At the highest layer of consideration, you should examine the beliefs and standards of your community. Think about what the community considers an acceptable gift – this would involve looking at both propriety and legality.

Giving someone a bottle of fine wine might be an acceptable reward in some communities, but in Saudi Arabia, it would be illegal. Make sure that you consider local laws and customs.

Also, take into account what the community would see as an acceptable gift. Regardless of legality, there are times when an otherwise legal reward would be seen as unacceptable. Community moral standards (*mores*) must be a factor in your selection.

Organizational Beliefs/Standards

In addition to the standards and beliefs of your community, you should also consider those of your organization. You should avoid rewarding in a fashion that could hurt the organization's image. Also, in many companies, there are restrictions as to the type of reward that can be given in a particular circumstance. In commercial circumstances, you should also avoid using a competitor's products as rewards.

Consider the case of Tracy, a social worker for a local charitable organization. Tracy is an amateur art historian, and all of those who work with her are aware of her love for classical art. Last year, she surpassed all of her targets at work, and her manager gave her a reward to recognize her accomplishment. Knowing of her love for classical art, her manager bought her a miniature replica of Michelangelo Buonarroti's classic statue, *David*, carved in soapstone. The statue depicts a nude male, with full exposure of the male genitalia.

Giving this reward breaks no laws. However, consider these additional details: the manager is a middle-aged, married male; Tracy is a thirty-something, single female; and the two work for the local Catholic Children's Aid Society. There could arise a scandal from this reward. Look at it from the eyes of some of the more devout members of the organization: an older married man buying suggestive statuary for a younger woman. In the eyes of this particular community, the gift is unacceptable, even if it is legal.

Image © 2003 Digital Michelangelo Project, and the Soprintendenza ai beni artistici e storici per le province di Firenze, Pistoia, e Prato

Individual Beliefs/Standards

Finally, you must consider the moral, religious, and other beliefs of both the giver of the award and the recipient. It is important that the giver feels comfortable giving the reward, that he or she does not feel a conflict between the reward and their own personal values, else body language (and other non-verbal communication) will reveal that his or her efforts at recognition are insincere. Similarly, you want to give a gift that the recipient will appreciate. There is no point in giving a reward that will not be valued, as it loses its impact.

Giving a reward that does not suit the recipient shows that the giver does not know the recipient well, and did not take the time to find out about his or her preferences. What is the point in giving an award that the recipient will not value? This is wasteful and can be insulting to the recipient.

Consider the personal beliefs of both parties. If either the giver or the recipient are avid vegetarians, then there is no point in giving a dinner for two at a local steakhouse. While the recipient may be able to pass along an unwanted reward to a friend, it still leaves the recipient without a reward that he or she can enjoy.

Remember that the reason we give rewards is to encourage recipients to continue an effective behaviour. If the reward we give is not valued by the recipient, then there is no positive reward to reinforce the behaviour. Also, since others may see that the reward was inappropriate (and perhaps thoughtless) we will lose the indirect spin-off benefits of motivating the recipient's coworkers to mimic effective behaviours.

Where possible, talk to the recipients or talk to their coworkers to find out about hobbies, personality, culture, personal values, and religious beliefs. Take the time to find out enough to suggest appropriate rewards.

Choose a reward that suits the accomplishment

Once you have narrowed down your list of potential rewards to a handful, you will need to make your final selection based upon the size of the accomplishment. A large, challenging accomplishment demands a larger reward than does one that was easier to achieve.

If the recipient worked very hard towards the accomplishment, then an appropriate reward for that behaviour requires a sizable reward. Giving this person a reward that he or she deems to be too small will minimize his or her efforts and may likely lead to insult. Coworkers will also notice the injustice and will not be motivated to imitate the successful behaviours.

Conversely, if a reward is seen by the recipient and the team as being too large for the accomplishment, then the recipient may feel (over time) that he or she earned such a large reward and will expect it in the future for similar small accomplishments. The other team members may feel offended if they believe that they have made similar or greater efforts that have gone unrewarded or that have received smaller rewards.

Try to determine if the recipient and the team will think that the accomplishment deserves a small or large reward. Then, look at your short list of rewards and select one that best matches the perceived size of the accomplishment. The size of the reward is not determined by its dollar amount. To make a small reward larger, you may want to try giving it in a public forum, or personalizing it with an inscription recognizing the specific behaviours you want to reinforce.

Tie the reward to the accomplishment

Once you have chosen an appropriate reward that is suited to the community, the organization, and both the giver and the recipient, and once you have have ensured that the reward suits the perceived size of the accomplishment, you will need to give the reward to the recipient. Here are two tips for ensuring that your reward has the greatest positive effect on the recipient and on the other team members.

First, you'll want to make sure that the reward is directly tied to the specific behaviours or accomplishment that you want to recognize. If you do not tie the reward to the specific accomplishment or behaviour you are trying to reinforce, then you are greatly reducing any impact the reward may have on motivation or performance.

One project manager interviewed for this book indicated that she had a draw at each weekly team meeting for a small prize (under ten dollars). Team members were eligible for this reward simply for having shown up to the meeting. While this may be an effective way of motivating team members to attend the meetings, it may not reward the real performers for more important behaviours you want to reinforce; team members who cannot attend because they are working hard on deliverables in an attempt to keep the project schedule commitments do not get rewarded as they are not at the meetings.

Try to tie the reward to the behaviour by choosing a reward that is related to the behaviour. If a team member has come up with a unique invention that will save the company money, then a reward such as a book on the life of Thomas Alva Edison inscribed by the company president mentioning the specific accomplishment of the recipient may have far greater value than the $20 cost of the book itself.

Give the award in a timely fashion

The second tip for giving an appropriate reward effectively is to give the reward in a timely fashion. Make sure that you minimize the delay between performing the effective behaviours and the reward that reinforces them.

If you wait too long after an achievement before granting a reward, the benefits may be lost. The recipient may have forgotten the specific behaviours that led to the accomplishment, since he or she may have adopted different behaviours in the mean time. In this fashion, you could be reinforcing the wrong behaviours.

An additional negative impact from waiting too long is a possible loss of morale. If someone accomplishes something truly outstanding, and you wait too long afterwards to grant an award recognizing his or her achievements, then the person could become discouraged in the mean time, reducing his or her performance and impacting team morale.

Lastly, if a reward is not tied well to the specific accomplishments, then a late reward could be seen as rewarding a later accomplishment. The problem with this, is that the earlier accomplishment could have been a greater one, but if the reward is seen as only rewarding the later accomplishment, then the recipient could feel cheated out of a well-deserved reward for the earlier performance. Also, if the difference between the two is dramatic, then the sense of injustice is magnified in the eyes of the recipient and his or her coworkers.

To make sure that your appropriately-selected reward generates the maximum direct and indirect benefits for the organization, clearly tie the reward directly to the accomplishment, and then give the reward in a timely fashion. Immediate feedback is the best way of positively reinforcing behaviours – make the timing of rewards work for you, not against you.

42

CHAPTER FOUR

Team Rewards versus Individual Rewards

When designing a rewards programme, look for opportunities to create team-based rewards to supplement your individual rewards. Team rewards are made up of two types:

- **Group Rewards.** A reward that is earned by a group of people working together as a team. The reward will be shared by the entire team.

- **Open Rewards.** An individual reward that is made available to everyone meeting specific criteria. Those who meet the criteria can each earn the reward for themselves.

Group rewards encourage individuals to work together as a team towards a common goal. They can be very powerful teaming motivators, and have driven many teams to very high levels of performance.

When designing individual rewards, do not focus solely on those that can only have one winner, such as top salesperson of the year, since such awards may discourage many individuals from trying to earn them. This is especially true for those who are not typically top performers; these people may feel that the reward is unattainable to them, and will not try to improve.

Individual rewards with only one winner can destroy teaming as well; instead, balance these awards with ones in which people try to beat their own individual targets, not those of their peers. Then there can be many winners, so more people will attempt them. We call these rewards Open Rewards. These open rewards help build up a sense of teaming, since staff will help each other to improve their performance and earn the rewards – the team members are not competing against each other, so they will be more likely to cooperate.

One project manager interviewed for this book indicated that he set up a contest with his project team. During the project, any deliverable that was completed earlier than its scheduled date earned the responsible team member points equal to the number of days it was delivered early. The points total for each team member was included in the weekly progress reports. At the end of the project, the top ten points earners received a reward. This was a very successful way of motivating the team, while still rewarding individuals for their specific performances.

PART TWO

101 Reward Ideas for $20 (or Less!)

CHAPTER FIVE

Reward Ideas

Once you have decided to give a reward, your next task is to find one that meets the four success criteria discussed in Chapter 3. You'll want to find a reward that suits the individual person, that is given in a timely fashion, and is tied to (and suitable for) the accomplishment or behaviour that you want to reinforce.

The most obvious reward possibility is cash. When giving cash, you'll have no conflicts over suitability to the person or the accomplishment. Cash is an obvious substitute for any other possible reward option. The one drawback with cash, however, is that it can seem impersonal. When giving rewards that have a smaller cash value, you should try to find a creative alternative to giving just cash, such as those under $20 rewards mentioned in this book. A reward of a $20 bill does not seem thoughtful and may not be valued as highly as an inscribed book by

the recipient's favourite author or a bottle of their favourite wine. In many cases, a reward item other than cash will be more highly valued and appreciated by the recipient than a more costly cash alternative; the trick is to choose the reward wisely.

The rewards in this book have been grouped into a number of categories:

- Ways of saying Thank You,

- Food and Drink,

- Certificates,

- Events and Entertainment,

- Trophies,

- Giftware and Gift Certificates,

- Time Off, and

- Negative Rewards.

Many of the rewards in this section of the book could fall into multiple categories. For simplicity, they are represented here in the category to which they are most suited.

Listing of reward ideas

Below is a list of reward ideas, sorted by reward category. More detailed explanations of the ideas are in the chapters that follow. While the book promises 101 reward ideas, some bonus ideas are included, bringing the total number of reward ideas in the book to 115.

Ways of Saying "Thank You"

1. Thank you note - from manager

2. Thank you note - from executive

3. Note of customer appreciation

4. Public praise

5. Private praise

6. Send a note home

7. Executive interview

8. Executive appearance

9. Notice board posting

10. Newsletter article

11. Letter of reference

12. Invitation to present at departmental meeting

13. Invitation to present at executive meeting

14. Birthday visit

15. Special assignments

Food and Drink

16. Pizza delivered to the office

17. Coupon for a pizza slice and a soda

18. Project closeout meal/party

19. Coffee and muffins

20. Doughnuts/pastries

21. Ice cream

22. Ice cream gift certificates

23. Restaurant gift certificates

24. Lunch with management

25. Team food day

26. Team lunch

27. Hydration station

28. Bottle of wine

29. Team cake

30. Project cookies - decorated cookies

31. Project cookies - jumbo fortune cookies

32. Summer treats

33. Smartie™ award

34. Chocolate treats - unique shaped chocolates

35. Chocolate treats - truffles with thank you letter

36. Life Saver™ award

37. Flowers

38. Bag-o-gold

Certificates

39. Top contributor certificate

40. Teaming excellence certificate

41. Customer appreciation certificate

42. High-demand skills award

43. Best meeting attendance award

44. Worst meeting joke award

45. Hero award

46. Superman/Superwoman award

Events and Entertainment

47. Movie breaks

48. Meeting mania - parks

49. Meeting mania - rooftops

50. Meeting mania - personal back yards

51. Paintball

52. Laser tag

53. Bowling

54. Sailing

55. Pool party

56. Mini golf

57. Driving range

58. Greens fee for a team member to go golfing

59. Karaoke night

60. Billiards tournament

61. Darts tournament

62. Soccer

63. Baseball

64. Volleyball

65. Winter sports - Tobogganing

66. Winter sports - Ice skating

67. Winter sports - Snowman building contest

68. After work pub nights

69. Spare events tickets

70. Family pass to the local zoo

71. Family pass to a local public swimming pool

72. Family pass to the local fair

Trophies

73. Plaques

74. Homemade trophies

75. Group photos

76. Signed baseball bat

77. Goofy trophies - Team mascott

78. Goofy trophies - Busy-as-a-Beaver/Bee Award

Giftware and Gift Certificates

79. Gift certificate from a bookstore

80. Book

81. Music

82. Movie tickets

83. Gift certificates for a hobby

84. Coffee mugs - team logo or slogan

85. Coffee mugs - personalized with award details

86. Leather business card holders

87. Personalized stationery

88. Engraved letter opener

89. Engraved paper weight

90. Museum tickets

91. Team T-shirt

92. Negotiated discounts

93. Squeezable stress toys

94. Personalized mouse pads

95. Teamwork movies on DVD or VHS

96. Gifts to children of team members

Time Off

97. Creative giveback time

98. Extra day off

99. Donate a day off

100. Day off for social good

101. Late start or leave early

102. Adjusted work days

103. Extended lunch breaks

104. Mentoring time

Negative Rewards

105. Negative certificates - Sillist mistake of the month

106. Negative certificates - Slow-poke award

107. Negative certificates - Lone wolf award

108. Negative certificates - Headless chicken award

109. Ugly neckties

109. Funny hats

110. Negative award T-shirts

111. Headbands with horns/halos, etc.

112. Rubber chicken

113. Giant rubber eraser

114. Plastic or rubber fish

115. Toilet seat certificate frame

CHAPTER SIX

The Power of "Thank You"

When discussing low-cost reward options, the most obvious is often the best. We do not say "thank you" enough to our coworkers. Simply by verbally recognizing someone's efforts or accomplishments, you can often achieve the same results as if you had given a physical reward of some kind.

Now, we must realize that thanking others is not easy for some people; they may feel that having to thank people means that you then owe them a favour, or that they are in some way superior, for they did something that the thanker could not do on his or her own. We need to help these people overcome such concerns.

Not only is a "thank you" inexpensive, but it can also be quite effective. As such, it should be one tool that is always in our rewards toolbox, ready to be used at a moment's notice. Liberally thanking others, in a sincere fashion, helps build team morale and contributes to a sense of cooperativeness.

> *I always find that a true thank you given face to face with a good handshake has great impact whether I receive it or whether I give it. This 'thank you' is probably the greatest part of the recognition. The gift which might be given at the same time just emphasizes the gesture.*
>
> Martin Rivest, Directeur de projets, personal communications with the author, 2002.

The key point to make here is sincerity. As mentioned in Chapter 3, non-verbal communications can undermine our message, if we do not believe what we are saying. To thank people and make them feel that you are truly grateful, you need to believe what you say, and be congruent in your verbal and non-verbal communications. In other words, "Thanks" doesn't work if you are faking it.

Below we will examine several ways to say "thank you" to your team members.

Thank you note

Thank a team member in writing and distribute the note to the broader team via email or by posting it on a team bulletin board. The note can be signed by the project manager, or, for added effect, the note can be signed by an executive of the organization. For added impact, make sure that the award recipient is aware that a copy of the note goes to his or her functional manager for inclusion in the individual's personnel file.

Customer appreciation

Sometimes, the most powerful praise one can receive is not from our managers, nor our peers, but rather from our cusomters. In many industries, customers are the final arbiters of what is acceptable behaviour from service providers. Presenting a note of praise signed by a customer that highlights the positive behaviours of your team can be the best way to say "thank you" and motivate team members.

Public praise

At a team or departmental meeting, describe the team member's specific actions that led to the reward, the positive results of those actions, and the importance of those results to the project or the company. Make sure that the recipient is in attendance. You may want to walk up to the recipient and shake his or her hand at the conclusion of your remarks.

Private praise

For those who are modest or shy, being praised publicly could be worse than having a root canal operation. If you suspect that the recipient could be uncomfortable with public recognition, then simply recognize them privately. Make a special trip to the recipient's desk and spend a minute thanking them for their accomplishment and note the specific behaviours that contributed towards the accomplishment.

Send a note home

Sometimes a more personal touch is better. Try writing a personal, hand-written note of thanks and send it to the recipient's home or office. It is not often these days that we take the time to write anything by hand, almost everything is typed into a computer and printed. This added personal touch will add an extra dimension to your recognition. Sending a note to someone's home might be appropriate if he or she had to sacrifice a significant amount of family time for the good of the project.

Executive interview

For those who make significant accomplishments, ask a senior executive to call the recipients on the phone, visit them at their desks, or ask that the employees stop by the executive's office. Once they are together, have the executive thank the recipients for their specific accomplishments. Coach the executive on the details so that he or she does not have to refer to notes while speaking – make it appear as if the accomplishment is recognized and important at the senior management levels. Give the recipient a chance to briefly discuss any issues or suggestions for improvement now that they have the ear of a senior executive. Sometimes this can be the most appreciated gift of all, having return benefits for the organization, in that a new idea for improvement might drive much greater organizational efficiencies and improve morale.

Executive appearance

For significant group accomplishments, consider having a senior executive stop by the next team meeting and talk about the achievements of the team, noting the specific behaviours that have led to the recent accomplishment. As noted before, brief the executive thoroughly so that he or she will know what to say without looking scripted.

Notice board posting

Some teams maintain a bulletin board of announcements and important memos. Try placing a note explaining the exemplary behaviour of a team member on the notice board with a word of thanks. Public recognition from peers motivates many people to great achievements.

Newsletter article

Where team bulletin boards are not available, many organizations use departmental, divisional, or project newsletters. Try including a short announcement of why the recipient is receiving the recognition, remembering to follow the four key criteria outlined in Chapter 3.

Letter of reference

For team members working on an employment contract, or for those working for a subcontracting company, a letter of reference praising their good work can be a treasured way to say "thank you." When looking for new contracts, they can use the letter of reference to thelp them get work, and a good letter of reference may be a useful tool to them for many years to come.

Invitation to present at departmental meeting

Some people treasure the opportunity to present at department or divisional meetings; such exposure helps them earn the recognition of their peers, and may open up future career opportunities for them. Be careful when making such an offer, however: not everyone wants to be in the spotlight.

Invitation to present at executive meeting

Similar to presenting at departmental meetings of peers, you may also offer the chance to present at meetings of executives within an organization. This gives the recipient a chance to increase his or her exposure at a high organizational level, perhaps creating an opportunity for advancement.

Birthday visit

Simply keeping track of the birthdays of employees and taking the time to stop by their desks and give them your best wishes is a simple, yet effective management behaviour. You can combine the visit with a "thank you" for the recipient's outstanding achievements.

Special assignments

You may also give an outstanding team member the opportunity to take a choice assignment. This may be some work that closely aligns with their personal interests, skills development goals, or career aspirations. Take the time to get to know your team members so that you may recognize these opportunities when they come along.

CHAPTER SEVEN

Food and Drink

One of the most common ways of rewarding others inexpensively is through food and drink. Everyone enjoys a good meal and has a favourite beverage. Food and drink make up the largest category of rewards suitable for all recipients.

When deciding on whether to give food or drink as a reward, consider the nature of the reward. If the accomplishment is something that is a once-in-a-lifetime achievement, or a career-defining moment, you will not want to reward with something that will be consumed and then is gone – you'll want something that will be a permanent reminder of the achievement and recognition. In such cases, consider giftware, trophies, certificates, and other non-consumables.

Another pitfall to avoid is the suitability of the food or drink reward in light of vegetarianism, religious food restrictions, dietary food restrictions, allergies, preferences, and other constraints. While it is hard to know exactly what a person does and does not like, you can at least make initial inquiries to determine if there are any general restrictions, and choose accordingly.

Pizza delivered to the office

For those who are working late at night, or over the dinner hour, consider having a pizza delivered to the office. You do not have to be there yourself, but it shows you are thinking of those still working away at their desks, which can help them feel appreciated. The "pizza break" will also give the team members a chance to relax and discuss personal matters rather than work, and improves team bonding.

Coupon for a pizza slice and a soda

For those who regularly work through their lunch hours, bringing in a pizza and sodas is a welcome reward. If you do not want to reward a group at once, then many pizza take-out restaurants offer coupons for a slice of pizza and a soda that you can purchase and hand out to the team for rewards. Giving out individual coupons has the added advantage that you do not require everyone to agree on toppings for the pizza like you would if you ordered a whole pizza for a group.

Project closeout meal/party

At the end of a project, many teams get together for a meal and/or a party. You can do this inexpensively if you hold the party at the office or at someone's home. You would provide the food for the meal, or the snacks, sodas, and music for the party. These types of events help foster a team comraderie that endures past the project completion. In our busy work lives, we do not get many chances to get together socially outside of work time. These meals/parties give us a chance to get to know our team members socially, and help build lasting team bonds and even friendships.

Coffee and muffins

When holding an early morning team meeting, providing coffee and muffins is a welcome treat for team members who may have had to get up extra early to make it in to work for the meeting. Many people need their caffeine to get started in the morning. Remember that not everyone likes coffee – provide tea for those non-coffee drinkers. Alternately, you could purchase a number of coffee and muffin coupons from a local coffee shop and give them out as inexpensive rewards for smaller accomplishments.

Doughnuts/pastries

An inexpensive way to provide a little treat in the morning for teams is to bring in a box of doughnuts or pastries. Pass the box around at team meetings, or place it in a central area and notify team members that the doughnuts are available for those who want to drop by and pick one up. This reward has become quite common in some companies and has since started to lose its effectiveness. If you are in such a company, try to choose another reward idea that is new to your team.

Ice cream

On hot summer days, nothing cools down better than an ice cream. You can bring in ice cream sandwiches or other ice cream treats for team events, or you can purchase coupons for a free cone from the local ice cream parlour.

Ice cream gift certificates

Many ice cream parlours sell gift certificates good for one ice cream cone. In the summer, these are quite popular, and only cost around $2 each. This might be a good choice if there is one of these places close to your place of work, so recipients can walk over on their lunch hours to pick up a treat.

Restaurant gift certificates

Why not present a gift certificate to a popular restaurant chain? You can gain added benefits by saying that the reward is for the recipient to take his or her spouse or "special someone" out in recognition of the sacrifices of personal time that the recipient made for the good of the project.

Lunch with management

An interesting twist to taking someone out to lunch, is to have the project manager, another senior manager, or an executive take a team member out to lunch and give him or her the air time to discuss any issues. You combine the rewards of a lunch, recognition, and a chance to "be heard" – a very beneficial combination for the recipient. These opportunities also can be very motivational to team members who have active issues they would like to pursue.

Team food day

Have a "food day" during a project and encourage all team members bring in some home-made food items from their respective cultural traditions to share with the team. This builds cultural awareness, expands people's horizons, and often leads to team building for multicultural teams. Best of all, it is nearly free – you need to supply only paper plates, napkins, and plastic utensils.

Team lunch

Host a team luncheon at one team member's home, or as a picnic in a local park. Team members can provide barbeque, sandwiches, fruit, and the like while the project or departmental budget supplements the contributions with drinks and desserts. Often, you can find nearby scenic parks with picnic tables to turn the lunch into a team outing.

Hydration station

Purchase a case of bottled water and a few cases of soda pop. Let team members come for free beverages while they are working on long, monotonous work. This is especially appreciated during the summer or in work environments that get hot and stuffy. Getting up to grab a drink gives team members a break from sitting and provides them with a networking opportunity.

Bottle of wine

For a more formal gift than a slice of pizza or some doughnuts, consider a bottle of wine gift wrapped and presented with a formal thank you in front of team members. Very good wines can be found for only a few dollars, and recipients usually appreciate them. Even those who do not drink themselves often appreciate such gifts as they can open them at their homes for guests or take them to dinner parties where others will be drinking wine.

For an interesting twist, if giving out a team reward, consider customized wine labels. Some smaller wineries, and most brew-your-own stores, sell self-adhesive blank wine labels that can be used in your computer printer. You can create a label recognizing the team and mentioning a specific achievement.

Team cake

Purchase (or bake yourself) a small cake for your team to celebrate special achievements. Don't forget remote team members, as they deserve a treat too, and often have difficulty feeling like part of the team. One person surveyed for this book used this to great success:

> I bought a cake, invited the management [and the local team members] and couriered pieces of cake to Montreal to my out of town team members. [The couriered cake] arrived at the specified time, in a box with a thank-you note, plates, forks, and napkins. We all celebrated together. [. . .] All team members were surprised, especially that everyone was thought of, and we all celebrated at the same time (over the phone) together. Our senior [management] congratulated everyone.[1]

Project cookies

Here is a chance for home bakers to make a special contribution. Bake large cookies decorated with the project

---

[1] *Shannon M. Regan, Project Management Process Owner for a large corporation, personal communications with the author, 2002.*

name, the team logo, or some other identifying mark, and
distribute them as individual rewards or to the team as a group
reward. You can decorate the cookies as award certificates with
phrases such as
"World's Hardest
Worker," "Top
Contributor," or
"Great Job!" Puns or
other silly phrases on
the cookies could
create a fun, relaxed
mood amongst the
team members.

An interesting variation to the cookie idea is to bake
jumbo fortune cookies and insert funny quotations that are
relevant to the project. These are good for group rewards.
People will have fun opening the cookies and will also have a
laugh at the contents. One project manager interviewed for
this book also admitted to putting small rewards in random
cookies; in his case, he inserted a new five dollar bill instead of
a funny quotation in two of the cookies. By doing this, he
added some suspense and the thrill of a prize to the team
reward experience.

Summer treats

A quick dash out to a corner store for a box of
Popsicles™ or ice cream sandwiches is a welcome treat on a hot
summer's day. Especially consider this if your team is working
outside or in hot conditions.

Smartie™ award

Give out a box of Smarties™ candy for the most thoughtful, innovative idea. In essence, playing on the word "smart" in the candy name to reward those who use their brains to solve problems during a project. This can be a lot of fun, especially if the award is a surprise given in front of a group, and if the reward idea has not been used before in the organization; usually, it evokes some laughter followed by applause.

Chocolate treats

Most cities have a chocolatier or chocolate factory that makes chocolate treats in almost any shape. You might be able to find a shape somewhat related to the project, or you can choose one suitable to a reward (a star, a heart, a "# 1" sign, or a dark chocolate plaque with white chocolate writing with the recipient's name, the date, and a description of the accomplishment or the name of the award.

Another idea for using chocolates as a reward is to print up a letter describing the achievement and thanking the recipient for their efforts. Then, glue or tape a wrapped chocoloate, or an individually-boxed chocolate truffle to the corner of the letter and present it to the recipient.

Life Saver™ award

Give a roll of Life Savers™ to the team member who went above and beyond the call of duty to help out another team member in trouble. Include a card noting the specific behaviour being recognized. You can have some fun presenting this reward and calling the recipient the "life saver" for his or her peers. This approach mixes praise and humour and can be a very effective and fun award to give in informal settings.

Flowers

While not technically food or drink, flowers are perishable gifts that are inexpensive and are often well-regarded by recipients. Consider a bouquet of flowers for team members you know may appreciate them. Make sure you tie the reward of flowers to a specific behaviour: roses given to someone may be misunderstood as a romantic advance.

The best suggestion I have learned [was] from our competition... I was sitting beside a guy from another tech company on a late night flight from Regina to Montreal. We both looked ragged after some long days. [. . .] He said that his company had sent flowers to his wife to thank her for the sacrifice of her time with her husband while he had an extended out of town stay on business.

Scott Steele, Manager, large corporation, personal communications with the author, 2001.

Bag-o-gold

Another possible food reward is the "bag-o-gold" idea. Get a small brightly-coloured cloth bag and fill it with edible gold coins. These coins are made from chocolate and are wrapped in gold foil to appear as if they were part of some pirate's treasure, and are available in many large candy stores.

Gold is the gift of vanity and common pride, but flowers are the gift of love and friendship.

Franz Grillparzer (1791–1872), Austrian poet, Phaon, in *Sappho*, act 2, sc. 5 (1819).

One should use praise to recognize what one is not.

Elias Canetti, Austrian novelist and philosopher. "1976," *The Secret Heart of the Clock: Notes, Aphorisms, Fragments 1973-1985* (1991).

CHAPTER EIGHT

Certificates

While a sincere "thank you" is the least expensive recognition one can give, there are many occasions where a permanent memento of that recognition is appropriate. The least expensive method of giving permanent recognition is the certificate.

Certificates come in many forms: individual achievement recognition, group achievement recognition, behaviour recognition, and negative recognition. The first types are discussed here, while the negative recognition certificates are discussed in Chapter 13.

Blank certificates may be purchased at any stationery store; they are made of quality paper with pre-printed borders or backgrounds. Many come with self-stick seals that may be applied and embossed with a corporate seal stamp for an added

effect. Often applying corporate seals to certificates makes them appear even more special, as we rarely see corporate seals applied to anything but legal documents these days.

The blank certificate stock can be printed (before applying seals) on inkjet or laser printers to include whatever text and logos or other graphics you require. The certificate text can be laid out in software applications such as MSWord, CorelDRAW, and Adobe PageMaker, or any one of a number of inexpensive certificate-making software packages. Your stationer may have one or more of these specialty software packages available near the display of blank certificate paper.

Top contributor certificate

You can award a certificate to the employee who goes above and beyond all others in helping achieve some important objective. This could be for helping the team meet a deadline, for working the most hours of uncompensated overtime, for sacrificing personal/family time for the project, or for the outstanding quality of his or her work. Be sure to use objective measures that are publicized to all – to do otherwise could jeopardize the secondary benefits of  motivating others to emulate the recipient, and could raise the spectre of favouritism and unfairness.

Teaming excellence certificate

This certificate can be given to those who make special efforts at helping other team members solve problems. Perhaps for being an excellent mentor, or teaching techniques to peers, or working well with team members from other business units. Awarding for this type of behavior encourages team bonding and synergy.

Customer appreciation certificate

Praise for a job well done means more when it comes from those paying for the work. This certificate can be given to the whole team, or just an individual, depending upon the circumstances. It is best when signed and presented by the project sponsor or customer. For some projects, you may want this "thank you" certificate signed by a number of key players from the sponsor's organization that the team worked with during the project.

High-demand skills awards

A certificate can be given out to those who are furthering their skills development by learning new techniques that are in high demand. Use of these skills for the first time on a project could earn a high-demand skills recognition award that thanks the recipient for taking the initiative to keep his or her skills up to date.

Best meeting attendance

Want to get people to show up to your meetings? Consider issuing an award for the best meeting attendance. This certificate would highlight those who are taking the meetings seriously. This award should be presented publicly in efforts to highlight to others the importance of good meeting attendance.

Worst meeting joke

Has anyone on your team ever told a joke before, during, or after a meeting that was a real "groaner" – a joke that was so bad that it was funny? If so, you may want to give out this certificate. Encourage humour whenever you can on projects; it helps reduce stress, builds team morale, and helps a team bond together. Recognizing attempts to bring humour to the project may build a more lighthearted attitude on your team.

Hero award

While good planning and sound project control can avoid most situations where heroic efforts are required to keep the project on track, sometimes such situations are unavoidable. In cases where the team members have worked over weekends, and worked "all-nighters," you can use this certificate as one way of recognizing their strong dedication and great efforts to help deliver a successful project.

Superman/Superwoman

For those individuals who have gone above and beyond the call of duty, print out a certificate identifying the recipient as a Superman or Superwoman for their dedication. For an added touch, you can adorn the certificate with self-adhesive superhero stickers.

Image © Adobe Systems Incorporated.

CHAPTER NINE

Events and Entertainment

A nother type of reward that will be appreciated by those who have worked very hard towards a recent accomplishment is an entertainment break or other similar event. Taking the time to stop and enjoy ourselves releases stress, gives the team an opportunity to bond, and encourages a healthy work-life balance.

Lower stress can lead to increased productivity and improved morale. In effect, rewarding a team member in this way benefits the recipient, other team members, and the organization as a whole. And it is fun too!

Movie breaks

To help foster team building and to reward a team for meeting a project objective, consider renting an upbeat, newly-released movie and playing it in a meeting room for the team. Show it on a television, or project it onto a large screen (or the wall!) using a data projector hooked up to the VCR or DVD player. Give the team two hours off to watch the movie, and

provide popcorn and sodas. You can
choose a newly released movie, or a
motivational one that shows
teamwork or individuals overcoming
significant challenges, such as *Apollo
13.*

Meeting mania

    Consider holding team meetings in unusual locations
for fun and stress relief. You can use public places such as parks
or rooftops, or (subject to your employer's policies) you may
use private facilities such as personal back yards for after-
meeting swimming pool parties. Especially when you have an
all-day meeting (such as a workshop or planning session),
consider alternative locations; if the team members are going to
be in your meeting all day, you will not have to worry about
what other meetings they may miss by attending your own off-
site meeting.

Paintball/Laser tag

    A popular team-building exercise in recent years is
paintball or laser tag. In these types of games, your team is
divided into two groups, and are each given a flag to protect at
opposite ends of an arena. Between the two groups is a course
filled with obstacles and hiding spots. Each team has the
objective of capturing the other team's flag while protecting
their own. Strategic thinking, teamwork, and risk taking are
encouraged in these games, while the team is out having fun
and blowing off stress. While the two sports are very similar,
paintball is more realistic, in that if a paintball hits any part of
your body, you are out of the game, while in laser tag you are

only out of the game if your chest-mounted sensor is hit. The advantage to laser tag, however, is that it does not hurt to be hit by the laser guns, while paintballs may lead to bruises, despite protective gear. Paintball can be quite messy too – team members will have to dress appropriately in old clothing.

Bowling

In most areas, bowling is still a relatively rare sport. Most people have tried it at least once in their lives, but few regularly play or have mastered the game. A fun outing for the whole team, bowling is an opportunity to do something different, something that is fun, non-violent, and in which everyone on the team will have an equal opportunity to shine. This fun sport will give the team lots of opportunities to bond and build new friendships.

Sailing

While preparing this book, a survey was sent out online to over 60,000 project managers around the world. One project manager who responded said that if his team completes their deliverables early in the morning of a key milestone date, then he takes them sailing on his boat for the rest of the afternoon. There is no cost, and the team gets to enjoy the fresh salt breeze and the warm sunshine.

Pool party

Consider having a pool party at a team member's home. Make sure you invite the entire team publicly, else problems may arise. On one project, a project manager invited the team members individually to his home for a pool party. The problem was that he started by inviting one of the team members he was working with on a Friday afternoon. She was an attractive, single woman. Over the weekend, she checked with other team members, but no one else had been invited yet. She felt very uneasy and thought that this was a ploy to get her alone in a bathing suit – perhaps a sexual advance; instead, at the following Tuesday team meeting, the project manager continued inviting the rest of the team members. When news of this reached the woman, she was relieved, but it did cause unnecessary tension. Be sensitive to these issues – invite people in groups to such events.

Mini golf for the team

Why not take the team out mini-golfing? This is a fun activity that equally challenges both men and women, and it is very inexpensive. You can find a mini-golf course with some very wacky and fun obstacles, or go for more authentic courses with real grass and natural hazards. Your team can be broken down into smaller subgroups who compete against all the other subgroups for a prize; this encourages team building, and allows you to assign individuals to a group along with others that they do not know, expanding their network of contacts.

Driving range outing for the team

Is your team suffering from frustration and tension due to project pressures? Here is an idea for a great stress reliever: take the whole team out to a driving range to practice their golf swings. Even those who have never played golf will have some fun. The cost is reasonable, and you can even split a bucket of balls between two or more team members. The real benefit is not the fun aspect, but rather the release of tension and frustration when team members hit those little white balls with their clubs. You can even have some fun putting little white stickers on some balls and then giving one or two to each team member, letting them write the name of a frustrating task, the logo of a company acting as a subcontractor, or even the title of the project on the sticker. Hitting these specially labeled balls can be very cathartic: a way for team members to release their pent up frustrations. Everyone will feel more relaxed afterwards, and may even share a few laughs over the banter generated by the names written on the labels. (I do not recommend allowing people to write the names of individuals on the balls – as tempting as this may be – as it promotes violence against others.)

Greens fee for a team member to go golfing.

For the individual who has accomplished something important, you may want to spring for the cost of the greens fee at a local public golf course. Some of the shorter (9-hole) executive courses cost under $20 a round, and may be played in a couple of hours. There may be the opportunity to combine this reward with an afternoon or morning off, providing the

recipient with time to golf. For the golf nut (and there are millions of them out there) this is a great gift; for those just learning, this could be a well-appreciated chance to practice.

Karaoke night

We secret shower singers all wonder if our singing sounds good *outside* of the bathroom, and in front of an audience. Taking your team out to a karaoke club is a chance for them to show their stuff on stage, in front of others. Even those who might be uncomfortable getting on stage will have fun at the event, laughing at the antics of others, and feeling a release of tension when they step down from the stage and walk back to their seats. This is a fun, non-competitive way to foster team bonding.

Billiards/Darts tournament

Another way for teams to relax and have some fun, billiards and darts are two games that require coordination and strategy rather than strength and endurance. As a result, they are excellent games for teams of mixed genders. Beginners will enjoy the games, and may play competitively with more skilled team members using a handicapping system. These are excellent games for use as team rewards, since they foster team bonding while at the same time stressing individual achievements.

Soccer/Baseball/Volleyball game

For larger teams, how about taking them to a local park and playing a game of soccer, baseball, or volleyball? The equipment costs for these games are minor, and many households already own the appropriate balls. The rules of these games can be simplified to help the players have fun, and to make them easier for those who are not very familiar with the games. Inter-team encouragement helps build positive relationships between players. Those who want to become leaders can practice their team building and coaching skills, bringing long term benefits to the project and the organization.

Winter sports

During the cold winter months, teams in snowy climates can take a break and enjoy some outdoor winter activities. Tobogganing, ice skating, or even a snowman-building contest can generate some fun and relieve stress for overworked team members. A welcome break, some fresh air, and mugs of hot cocoa afterwards can all be accomplished in only an hour or so, and the only out of pocket expense is the cocoa.

After work pub nights

My colleagues in the United Kingdom suggest getting the team together for a beer and some finger foods. Sharing a drink in an amicable atmosphere helps people let their guards down, and share some of their personal feelings that may not come out during the course of a project. This is a good opportunity for team members to vent their frustrations, share their pains, and offer support for each other. Of course, the beer drinking would have to start after company hours – we wouldn't want tipsy team members working on our critical activities.

Spare events tickets

In many organizations, salespeople get tickets to sports and entertainment events in order to take customers to the events. Many times, these tickets are not being used by the salespeople and are available for use by other employees. When such fortunate circumstances occur, try to obtain the tickets for use as rewards within your team. Usually, there is no cost for the tickets, and team members see them as special treats.

Family pass to the local zoo

A very inexpensive entertainment venue is the local zoo. Usually, one-day family passes can be purchased for under $20 for use as awards to team members with young children. This provides a learning opportunity for the children who always enjoy zoo visits.

Image © Adobe Systems Incorporated.

Family pass to a local public swimming pool

On a hot summer day, consider distributing a one-day family pass to the local public swimming pool. A family pass is only a few dollars, and can provide a welcome escape from the sun.

Family pass to the local fair

Many counties and towns have one or more local fairs (or circuses) that are held during the year. Some, such as harvest fairs, are held at specific times of the year, while others, such as circuses, can appear at almost any time. If you know the local fair is coming soon, inquire into the availability of one-day family passes for use as rewards for your team.

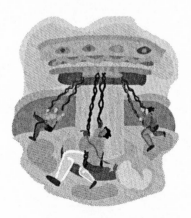

CHAPTER TEN

Trophies

For many accomplishments, consumable rewards (food, drink, events, etc.) are appropriate; however, for other accomplishments, more lasting mementos are in order. For long-lasting rewards, you can consider certificates and trophies. Certificates were discussed in Chapter 8; here we will discuss trophies.

For many people, trophies represent their most valued rewards. Like the Oscar trophies given out to the top people in the movie industry, you can create trophies to reward your team members for stellar achievements. As one of the most valued rewards, trophies should only be given for the most important achievements, and they should only be given publicly in front of the whole team (or organization!). Finally, the trophies should be given with some element of drama, building up to the presenting of the award: tell the story behind the award, describe the field of candidates, explain why the recipient was considered the best, and then give the award.

All that being said, there is a role for humour when presenting trophies. Some trophies, by their very nature, are farcical and meant to create laughs while still recognizing the recipient's achievements at the same time. When choosing a trophy, consider the formality of the event, the formality of

your relationship with the recipient, and
the nature of the accomplishment before
deciding whether to present a formal or
humourous trophy.

Plaques

A more enduring form of certificate, plaques add a
patina of richness and formality to their presentation. Be
careful when selecting plaques as your reward option that the
reward is one that the recipient will want to display on their
wall for years to come – there is no point in presenting a plaque
for recognizing an achievement of a temporary or transitory
nature. Overuse of plaques for these non-enduring
accomplishments can eventually diminish the value of future
plaques, as old ones will end up in drawers – forgotten – when
replaced by plaques for more recent accomplishments. Blank
plaques can be purchased and custom engraved at any
engravers, or you can purchase others upon which you can
mount a paper certificate to make it more enduring and formal.

Homemade trophies

Trophies do not
necessarily have to be purchased.
Using the technology, tools, and
craft skills of the team, you can
create a trophy that identifies the
project in some way. Make it out
of inexpensive materials, if
possible, and you will still get the
same impact without the
associated cost. Ideas for these

trophies include carved plaques, and statues made out of old CD-ROMs.

Group Photos

For a very inexpensive reward, try using a digital camera to take a photo of the team after a major accomplishment. Then, either send the photo via email or as a colour printout to each team member as a memento of the project, perhaps adding some text above and below the photo highlighting the accomplishment. People love to receive these photos, so that they can relive their glories in years to come.

Signed baseball bat

For the team member who "went to bat" for the team, get a baseball bat and have it signed by all team members for presentation in a public forum. You can also do this with a miniature baseball bat that you later mount on a plaque with a small brass plate indicating the title of the award, the recipient's name, and the date awarded.

Goofy trophies

On a more humourous note, many project managers adopt a stuffed animal as the project mascot. The PM calls out the top performer from the previous week during a project team meeting, and hands over the mascot to be his or her

"trophy" until the next
weekly team meeting.
You can get creative with
the trophy animals; for
example, you could use a
stuffed beaver for the
"Busy-as-a-Beaver
Award." (For those in
areas where beavers are
not familiar animals, you
can use a stuffed bee and

call it the "Busy-as-a-Bee Award.") While humour is welcome
with these "goofy" rewards, be careful not to cross the line into
awards that cause offense; Chapter 13 discusses the appropriate
use of negative rewards for your team members.

*Melvin the Moose - This started informally, when one employee
brought Melvin back from a trip and "awarded" him to a fellow
employee. Melvin is a stuffed moose that visits a different employee
each week. He is accompanied by an e-mail sent out to the team
explaining why he chose to visit a particular employee on a given
week, such as a particular project accomplishment, going out of
your way to help a team member, etc. Whoever gets him one week
has to find someone to send him to for the next week. It sounds
corny, but I am amazed at how glad people are to have Melvin's
company!*

Mary Mirus, project manager, personal communications
with the author 2001.

CHAPTER ELEVEN

Giftware and Gift Certificates

Perhaps the largest category of potential rewards is giftware. There are endless possibilities for modest gifts that recognize someone's performance, from fancy pens to books and music. Below are a few suggestions, but use your own creativity to come up with unique ideas.

Where a person's tastes are not well known, do not give gifts where personal tastes will likely have a large impact, such as music CDs. In cases like this, purchase a gift certificate from a well-known retailer instead. Make sure the retailer has several convenient locations, or else the recipient may be inconvenienced traveling to the retailer to redeem the gift certificate.

Gift certificate from a bookstore

Giving a gift certificate from a bookstore promotes literacy, learning, and is seen as more permanent and more valued than a gift certificate for a meal. Most people still value books, even if they have little time for reading in their busy lives. Books are always appropriate gifts. For those too busy to go shopping, or who do not live in the area, consider gift certificates from online book sellers, such as Amazon.com.

Book

Select a book on a topic of personal interest to the recipient and inscribe a note of thanks to the individual in the front cover. If you don't know the person well enough, try choosing a book about reaching goals, being successful, or something business or technology-related. Perhaps, you may want to have it hand signed by the sponsor or some other senior executive, and present it publicly to the recipient.

Music

Everyone loves music. While tastes vary between people, there is almost a universal appreciation for good music. If you know a person's music tastes, try presenting a newly-released CD from their favourite artist. Or, if you are not sure of their tastes, a safe bet is a gift certificate from a popular music retailer. Don't forget that CDs can be ordered online too, so consider a gift certificate from Amazon.com.

Movie tickets

A good escape from the pressures of our busy work lives, movies are a popular way to relax. One inexpensive reward you can give is a pair of tickets (or a gift certificate for the same) to a popular movie. Always give the tickets in pairs – no one likes to go to the movies alone. In many theatre chains, you can purchase a gift certificate that includes two movie admissions, popcorn, and drinks for under $20.

Gift certificates for a hobby

If you know a team member just moved in to a new house, or if they practice woodworking as a hobby, consider giving them a gift certificate to Home Depot (tools, materials), or Sears (tools, house wares), or some similar national chain. If you know an employee has a personal hobby, see if you can find a local store supplying such hobbyists that offers gift certificates. The recipients will appreciate the time you took to get an interest-appropriate gift.

Team coffee mugs

Coffee mugs can be inexpensively printed with custom logos or slogans. For example, you can get one printed with the name of the project, the team's logo or slogan, or have one personalized with the name of a team member and a statement about how they have excelled.

You could even combine the coffee mug with some of the ideas in Chapter 8 "Certificates." In this case, you would have the mug printed with statements such as "Top Contributor Award" or "Perfect Meeting Attendance Award, June 2004."

Leather business card holders

One unusual idea for an inexpensive reward is to have some leather (or leatherette) business card holders embossed with the team or company logo, or even the name of the project. These could be awarded to the team for making a major milestone date or exceeding quality targets, or for any similar group achievement.

Personalized stationery

You can always personalize items such as stationery. For example, you could award a notepad saying "From the desk of the world's best technician, Bob." Similar ideas include a pen engraved with the recipient's name, or Post-It™ notes printed with a statement of award, such as "Marian, 2003 Top Contributor."

Engraved letter opener or paper weight

Letter openers or paper weights can be purchased for only a dollar or two at discount stores. Have a number of these inexpensive items engraved with the name of the project and a word of thanks, for presentation to the project team. They can also be engraved with names and achievements for recognition of specific individuals.

Museum tickets

An inexpensive, yet unusual gift that you can award to a recipient is a family pass to a local museum. Museums usually have something for everyone in the family, and they are quite educational.

Team T-shirt

Why not have team T-shirts printed with the project name? Perhaps have them printed with a message saying "Product Name Version 2 - Successfully delivered on time" or some other phrase denoting an important accomplishment.

Negotiated discounts

If the project is for a retailer, or a company offering special services to the public, arrange a transferable discount certificate for team members. If the discount certificates are transferable, then recipients can gift them to family or friends who may be better able to use the discounts. Often, these discounts can be easily secured by asking the project sponsor. There is usually no cost for this reward, but these discounts are generally much appreciated by recipients.

Image © Adobe Systems Incorporated.

Squeezable stress toys

The recent craze for office stress toys has opened up a whole world of possibilities. You can purchase standard squeezable toys shaped like computers, Dilbert's™ boss, the heads of famous people, or many other things. Some promotional novelty vendors will even take orders for custom-shaped or custom-printed foam stress toys that you can have printed with the name of your project.

Personalized team mouse pads

Consider having a computer mouse pad printed with a picture of the recipient or his or her children, or with a team picture and the name of the project for a group award. Some computer stores now sell kits where you can insert colour printouts into a self-adhesive mouse pad surface covering, allowing you to make any mouse pad you desire, inexpensively and quickly.

Teamwork movies

Aside from showing movies to your team as a relaxation medium, consider awarding video cassette or DVD copies of movies demonstrating teamwork, such as *Apollo 13*. With this, you combine the idea of a reward with a motivational message and good role modeling opportunities.

Gifts to children of team members

When team members have been working long hours towards helping meet an important deadline, often they sacrifice some of their time at home with their children in order to get their work done. In these situations, special recognition of the sacrifices made by the family can be very effective. Look for opportunities to give small gifts to children of team members who have been working evenings or weekends. Along with the gifts, include a note thanking them for their sacrifices of mommy or daddy's time.

Image © Adobe Systems Incorporated.

CHAPTER TWELVE

Time Off

W hen team members "burn the midnight oil" to help make deadlines, sacrificing their own personal time, you should consider the possibility of giving them time off as a reward for their efforts and dedication. This will allow them to relax, catch up on the personal business that they could not attend to while working overtime on the project, and spend valued time with their loved ones. Some of the ideas presented in this chapter even structure the time off in a way that it also delivers benefits to the less fortunate members of our society.

Time off may not cost you anything, depending upon how labour costs are accounted for within your organization; regardless, time off is always worth considering. Time off allows us to rejuvenate, consider creative solutions to nagging problems, and it makes us generally more productive employees.

Creative giveback time

When a team member meets a significant milestone date, or completes an important deliverable, if there is some slack (or "down") time before the next activity must start, consider giving the person time to use his or her creativity to come up with ways of improving performance. This time could be spent documenting lessons learned to be used as input into future planning activities, teaching others how to perform some technique that the award recipient has mastered, or coming up with process improvements for the project or for individual work activities. Not only is this reward a great morale booster, but it can also lead to performance improvements that impact organizational or project profitability.

Grant an extra day off

If key team members have been working very hard to help meet a key milestone date, consider giving them an extra day off if the date is met. You may give them the break immediately upon achieving their goal, or you may ask them to schedule it later, if you are in the middle of a very busy period in your project.

Donate a day off

If you are having trouble getting authorization for a team member to take an additional day off, try donating one of your own. Simply come in to work one day, but claim it as a vacation day, and let your team member take a day off and

102

claim it as a work day. In this manner, you can avoid many of the problems that other time off arrangements have created for the human resources and payroll departments. The drawback is that you lose a day of your own vacation.

Day off for social good

Give the team a day off from their regular work duties and organize a volunteer activity that benefits society. Have them volunteer at a food bank, clean up a dirty roadside, deliver food boxes to the poor, or some other charity work on company time. This gives the team a break from their hectic work schedule, a chance to bond in a relaxed atmosphere, and a chance to help others who are less fortunate.

Late start or leave early

Something that should not cost you anything is to grant someone the right to come in to work one hour later, or leave one hour earlier for a period of time, perhaps one week. The reduction in work hours is minimal, and the improved employee morale may result in no loss of productivity with the reduced work hours. Employees with children will appreciate the chance to drop them off or pick them up from school, or the chance to spend some quality time with them after they come home from school.

Adjusted work days

Another idea that will improve employee morale and may not cost you anything is to adjust the schedule of planned work activities so that a rewarded employee's requested vacation days can be approved. This is useful in organizations that may not allow vacations during busy periods of time. Making an exception for an employee, in the form of a reward, leads to improved morale and can motivate the entire team.

Extended lunch breaks

Allow recipients to take extended (2 hour) lunch breaks. This gives them enough time to really enjoy a meal, attend to personal banking, go shopping, or other personal matters that will improve their work/life balance.

Mentoring time

Give team members some time off of their regular work activities to work with less experienced employees in the role of a mentor. This provides a double value: the employee gets a change of pace, allowing him or her to share experiences and teach others; at the same time, the organization benefits by having newer employees trained and lessons learned being shared, improving future performance.

CHAPTER THIRTEEN

Negative Rewards

Sometimes, one of the most effective ways to encourage people to change their behaviours is to gently ridicule the current behaviours that you find ineffective. In discussions with managers, I have heard many tales of gently goading team members to excellent performance. Public embarrassment can be a powerful motivator, but can also be very destructive. Using these "negative reward" techniques is a double-edged sword: they can help encourage someone to better performance, or they can demotivate and hurt the recipient, exacerbating the already negative behaviours you are trying to change.

This technique only works if the recipient has a good sense of humour and feels safe, in a trusting environment. Also, in advance of using these techniques, you should introduce the selected reward to the entire team in an informal group gathering, making sure you stress the humour and fun in the rewards, so that they do not come as a surprise. If you get negative feedback from the group, then do not proceed using these negative rewards. They are meant to be fun, but if everyone is not enjoying them, then they should not be used.

We cannot stress enough that these techniques are not for every team, nor for every project – you must be very sensitive to the dynamics of your own team and the feelings of individuals on the team. Use these techniques cautiously.

Negative certificates

These are certificates as described in Chapter 8; however, there is a catch: the printing on the certificate points out (in a funny way, of course) a negative behaviour. Examples of these certificates include

- Silliest mistake of the month;

- Slow-Poke Award for missed deadlines;

- Lone Wolf Award for team members who failed at some minor task because they tried to do it alone without asking for help; or

- Headless Chicken Award for team members who are frantically working away to meet looming deadlines, but are making mistakes because they are not taking the time to think things through (usually accompanied by a humorous cartoon graphic). This puts to action the old saying "running around like a chicken with its head cut off."

Ugly neckties

For an unusual spin on the award idea, consider giving a tacky, ugly, horribly unfashionable necktie to the team member who misses a performance objective for the week by the greatest amount. The recipient will have to wear the necktie for the week until the next team meeting, or at least *to* the next team meeting. Variations of this include

- Funny hats such as baseball caps with appropriate slogans, or Viking helmets with large horns;

- T-shirts with appropriate slogans on the front; or

- Headbands with horns, halos, or other funny attachments.

Rubber chicken

This reward idea embodies the concept of a funny trophy highlighting negative behaviour. This type of trophy is usually awarded to the team member who makes a careless mistake of some kind. If you use a rubber chicken, the recipient must hang the chicken over their desk for the week, before it is taken down and awarded to another team member at the next weekly meeting. In addition to the old rubber chicken idea, you can also use a number of other items:

- A giant rubber eraser inscribed with a description of the careless mistake;

- A plastic or rubber fish (such as a flounder or fluke); or

- A plastic toilet seat framing a description of why the award was given.

CHAPTER FOURTEEN

Conclusion

There is no point in giving rewards that will offend the recipients. Similarly, you will not gain any benefit from giving rewards in an ineffective manner. An effective rewards programme requires that you select rewards that are appropriate for the recipients, are clearly tied to specific behaviours that you want to encourage, and are presented in a way that maximizes the benefits to the organization.

Four Tips to Choosing the Right Reward

1. Choose a reward that suits the person
2. Choose a reward that suits the accomplishment
3. Tie the reward to the accomplishment
4. Give the reward in a timely fashion

You should maximize the return on every reward dollar you spend by ensuring the rewards deliver direct and indirect benefits in a cost-effective way. Direct beneifts are the motivating and supporting effects that rewards have on recipients. Indirect benefits are the spin-off effects on other people that see the recipients receiving rewards tied to specific behaviours; those affected indirectly may seek to mimic the successful behaviours of the recipients, producing broader returns for the organization. Tally up these direct and indirect benefits and select a reward option that will deliver these benefits in a cost-effective manner. This book is full of inexpensive ways of rewarding individuals and groups that, if used correctly, will help deliver those benefits.

While this book contains many ideas for inexpensive or no-cost rewards, it does not exhaust the topic. I am amazed at the creative ideas that managers come up with to reward employees while under tight fiscal constraints. If you have any new ideas to add to this book, or have some interesting annecdotes to share, please feel free to send them to the author at aguanno@sympatico.ca for use in future editions of this book.

Bibliography

Aguanno, Kevin. "Low-Cost Ways to Reward your Project Team Members." *Inside Project Management.* 3:11 November 2003 pp. 14-16.

David, Matthew and Aguanno, Kevin. "Motivating Team Members During Tough Times." *Inside Project Management.* 3:11 November 2003 pp. 5-6.

Deeprose, Donna. *How to Recognize and Reward Employees.* New York: American Management Association (AMACOM), 1994.

Hale, Roger L. and Rita F. Maehling. *Recognition Redefined: Building Self-Esteem at Work.* Exeter, New Hampshire: Monochrome Press, 1993.

Klubnik, Joan. *Rewarding and Recognizing Employees: Ideas for Individuals, Teams, and Managers.* New York: McGraw-Hill, 1995.

Kohn, Alfie. *Punished by Rewards: The Trouble with Gold Stars, Incentive Plans, A's, Praise, and Other Bribes.* Houghton Mifflin, 1999.

Nelson, Bob. *1001 Ways to Increase Your Return on People: Motivating, Energizing, and Inspiring Today's Workplace.* Site Coordinator's Guide for an educational television broadcast on PBS: The Business Channel, 30

September 1999. Washington: National
Technological University, 1999. Guide available at
http://www.ntu.edu/notes/busmanchannel/notes/
WAYS0000_sg.pdf. Also see <http://www.nelson-
motivation.com/> and <http://www.amazon.com/
bobnelson/>.

- - -. *1001 Ways to Reward Employees.* New York: Workman
Publishing, 1994.

- - -. *101 of the Best No-Cost & Low-Cost Ways to Reward
Employees.* San Diego: Nelson Motivation Inc., 2002.

- - -. "Be Creative When Rewarding Employees." San Diego:
Nelson Motivation Inc., 2002.

Urquhart, Jody. "Caught in the Act." Gantthead.com Web
site. 2 Jan 2002. 14 Feb 2002 <http://
www.gantthead.com/article/1,1380,74342,00.html>.

Wilson, Thomas B. *Innovative Reward Systems for the Changing
Workplace.* New York: McGraw-Hill, 1994.

About the Author

Kevin Aguanno is a driven, result-oriented solutions designer and project manager with over seventeen years of experience working with a wide range of industries. He is the past Executive Producer of IBM Canada's Interactive Media Studio, and Principal of IBM Canada's Media & Entertainment Industry unit.

Mr. Aguanno specializes in managing complex application development and systems integration projects. One of his most recent projects featured hundreds of developers working from seventeen locations around the world, integrating products from several vendors that had never been integrated before. He has been brought in as a trouble shooter to turn around many troubled application development and systems integration projects, and is known in the industry for this expertise. He has spoken at conferences and has published

Photographer: Gallery 282, Oshawa, ON, Canada.

113

articles on managing complex projects.

His knowledge and competency as a project manager are certified by IBM and PMI, and he is a member of both PMI and the Association for Project Management in the U.K. Winner of several international awards, Mr. Aguanno is a proven manager and public speaker active in research and writing on the topic of project management.

Kevin is the editor of *Inside Project Management*, an Element-K journal, and has written four books. His two most recent books are *Beyond the PMP: Advanced Project Management Certification Options*, and *101 Ways to Reward Your Project Team for $20 (or Less!)* His articles appear regularly in various professional journals.

Author's Web site: **www.mmpubs.com/aguanno**

Speaking Services

      Kevin Aguanno is available to speak at association and corporate events. Delivery via teleconferences, Web-delivered seminars, 1-2 hour keynote speeches, and either half or full-day workshops. Available topics include:

- Project Management

- Project Closeout Best Practices

- Agile Development Methods

- Internet Technology

- Rewarding for Performance

For additional details contact his agent at speakers@mmpubs.com or visit the URL www.mmpubs.com/aguanno/speaking.html

**2.5 hour
Seminar**

For additional details
on this seminar, and for
other booking
information, contact
speakers@mmpubs.com
or visit the Web site at
www.mmpubs.com/
aguanno/speaking.html

Ever-Changing Requirements? Use Agile Methods to Reduce Project Risk

This tutorial will outline the underlying principles of Agile Development and the details of how it differs from traditional development projects. It examines the practical applicaiton of some common agile techniques, sharing lessons learned from real projects.

An extension of Mr. Aguanno's often-requested presentation "Agile Development Using Scrum," this new presentation includes a comparisson of other agile development methods, including Extreme Programming, Crystal Method, and Feature Driven Development, among others. The seminar is peppered with lively stories from Mr. Aguanno's experiences delivering real-world agile development projects.

Participants will come away from the presentation with a high-level understanding of the Agile Development philosophy and how it differs from traditional development approaches, a high-level familiarity with a number of available agile methods, an understanding of how to apply some agile techniques on their own projects, and the ability to determine when those techniques are appropriate.

1 hour Presentation
For additional details on this presentation, and for other booking information, contact speakers@mmpubs.com or visit the Web site at www.mmpubs.com/aguanno/speaking.html

Project Closeout Best Practices

Project closeout always presents challenges: getting final approvals, administrative closure, contract closure, capturing lessons learned, and others. In a world moving at the speed of e-business, efficient project closure is a must and may even give you a competitive edge.

Based upon three years of research, this presentation outlines the best practices for closing out projects with an innovative model combining the best features from many different project management methodologies. Participants will also receive a project closeout checklist they can use to ensure they have not missed any critical items when closing out their own projects.

Kevin Aguanno has presented this topic to thousands of project managers around the world at conferences such as ProjectWorld, and via international teleconferences and Webinars. The presentation is rich with content, and can be extended to 90 minutes by allowing more time for questions after the presentation. This topic always generates lively discussions with audience members sharing their own anecdotes and lessons learned.

So, You Think You're Done?

What to do after the launch.

Getting to final sign-off on a project is a major hurdle. Your job is almost done ... or is it? This tape shows you how to obtain sign-off and maps out the necessary project closeout activities.

Kevin Aguanno

The PM Essentials Library

Getting to final sign-off on a project is a major hurdle. Your job is almost done ... or is it?

Project closeout always presents challenges: getting final approvals, administrative closure, contract closure, capturing lessons learned, and others. In a world moving at the speed of e-business, efficient project closure is a must and may even give you a competitive edge.

Based upon 3 years of research, this tape outlines the best practices for closing out projects with an innovative model combining the best features from many different project management methodologies. This tape will show you how to get an easier sign off from customers and then maps out all of the project closeout activities you may need to consider.

Audio Cassette $12.00   ISBN 1-895186-10-2

Published in 2003 by Multi-Media Publications Inc., R.R. #4B, Lakefield, ON, Canada, K0L 2H0.   Order online at www.mmpubs.com/aguanno/tape2.html

How would you like to deliver projects more quickly and with greater customer satisfaction in an environment of frequent scope changes?

Based on a live recording of a presentation Mr. Aguanno has delivered many times to project managers and software developers in Canada, the U.S., Europe, Asia, and Australia. One of his most popular presentations.

This presentation outlines the underlying principles of Agile Development and details of how it differs from traditional development projects. Then, using an agile project management method called Scrum, it illustrates how agile management methods used in software development may be extended to projects from other application areas outside of information technology. Participants will come away from the presentation with a high-level understanding of the Agile Development philosophy and how it differs from traditional development approaches, enough of an understanding of Scrum to be able to determine if and how it could be implemented on a project, and a list of resources for further information on Agile Development and Scrum.

Audio Cassette $12.00   ISBN 1-895186-08-0

Published in 2003 by Multi-Media Publications Inc., R.R. #4B, Lakefield, ON, Canada, K0L 2H0.   Order online at www.mmpubs.com/aguanno/tape1.html

Time Management for Students

This award-winning multimedia CD-ROM teaches students how better to manage their time, which studies show reduces stress, improves grades, and helps students achieve their goals. Jam-packed with step-by-step instructions and relevant examples, this CD-ROM uses some of the latest techniques to teach time management skills to students. The instruction uses multi-modal teaching to help students learn through hearing, reading, and interacting in live examples.

Throughout the learning, your progress is tracked, and advanced hyperlinking and bookmarking features allow you to move to the topics of most interest to you. At the end, the CD-ROM will link you to a Web site where you can access and download time management tools for your own use. The Web site will also point you to other time management resources on the Internet.

Time management is among the most important of student skills. Research shows that improving your ability to manage time can improve your grades at school substantially, can help you reduce stress, and help you achieve your goals. Don't allow poor time management skills to get in the way of your grades, your confidence, or your success.

PC (Windows) CD-ROM $29.00

Published in 1999 by York University, Toronto, Ontario, Canada. Order online at www.mmpubs.com/aguanno/cd1.html

Beyond the PMP

Advanced Project Management Certification Options

Kevin Aguanno

The Project Management Essentials Library

Want more $$$ money?

How about the prestige that comes from that promotion you've wanted?

Many think that once you've earned your Project Management Professional (PMP) designation from PMI, you've achieved the top project management qualification. In this book, Kevin Aguanno presents a whole world of additional qualifications that build on the PMP. The PMP is not the end — it is the beginning of lifelong PM skills development.

Highlighting the distinction between knowledge-based qualifications (like the PMP) and competency-based qualifications, *Beyond the PMP* is also a reference book, containing detailed information on many PM degree and certificate programmes from around the world, as well as information on available competency-based certifications.

This book is an essential reference for beginning and advanced PMs who are planning their skills development and career advancement. Get it now to help you prepare your own career development plan.

A sample from the book's introduction appears on the following pages.

Free Bonus!

The following is a sample taken from the introductory chapter of *Beyond the PMP: Advanced Project Management Certification Options* by Kevin Aguanno.

Introduction

The Project Management Professional (PMP®) certification from the Project Management Institute (PMI) has grown rapidly to become a major project management qualification in North America and is making inroads in other parts of the world; yet, many who have attained this qualification are now wondering "What next?" Project management training organizations and publications focus on providing the skills and knowledge required for attaining the PMP certification, but since there is little public discussion of qualifications beyond the PMP, few have knowledge of what further qualifications can be attained in project management.

Rapid growth has seen the number of PMPs jump from the start of the qualification in the 1980s to approximately 10,000 in January 2000 and to a total of 46,890 in May of 2002. Recently, China has said that it aims to certify an additional 50,000 new PMPs before the start of the 2008 Beijing Olympics. Such growth has been driven by the active promotion of the qualification by PMI and the lack of other widely-available PM qualifications in North America. This growing body of PMPs is now creating a demand for additional education and qualification opportunities. One result is the proliferation of project management certificate and degree programmes offered by universities around the world. PMI itself has tried to address the issue through the development of its now defunct Certificates of Added Qualification (CAQ) that essentially provide a method of certifying a candidate with an area of specialty beyond the general project management knowledge assessed by the PMP exam. PMI has also developed a qualification below the PMP for those beginning in the field called the Certified Associate in Project Management (CAPM) but this addresses the needs of novices involved in the project management profession, not those seeking advanced qualifications.

In addition, employers have been starting to question the real skills and capabilities that individual project managers bring to the workplace. There is no guarantee that having some of these qualifications will mean that an employee will deliver projects successfully; some of these qualifications only test the ability of the candidate to remember some key facts, not their ability to apply them successfully in the workplace.

Employees are starting to feel this new pressure being applied by business and are looking for additional qualifications that demonstrate their ability to apply effectively their specialized knowledge. There has been a burst of specialty qualifications appearing on the marketplace to address this growing demand, some of which are project management-related qualifications.

Certainly, having *any* qualification does not guarantee work. While the marketplace may demand that job candidates possess certain qualifications, employers are also looking at past experience and personal attitude as hiring criteria. David I. Cleland, Professor Emeritus of the Univeristy of Pittsburgh, supports this position:

> **Certification, degrees, and other qualifications are just hunting licenses. They do not guarantee anyone work, but give a person the right to hunt for that work.**[1]

What's Next?

Up until recently, project managers have viewed the PMP as the end goal of their career development; they have taken courses, documented their project experiences, and studied hard for the exam – all of their efforts focused on attaining those three magic letters after their name: *PMP*.[2] Now, the growing body of project managers with freshly-printed PMP certificates hanging on their walls is coming to the realization that attaining the PMP is not the end of their career development; there is still much to learn and increasing job competition among PMPs.

While the PMP was seen, for several years, as the top award in project management (at least in North America), now people are seeing it as one milestone in a lifelong project management career development journey. One project manager, Glen Maxfield of the Canadian Wheat Board, sums it up nicely:

> **Practically speaking, the PMP is an entry-level standard. I've got one, and it wasn't**

hard. Not everyone is going to have the ability to "beat" the test without any actual knowledge, [. . .] although no doubt a few leakers will get by. Like any other paper certification [. . .] it's no guarantee of success. I don't think I can say this strongly enough, but anyone who thinks that having a PMP transforms them into an infallible being is, in fact, a fool.

I find that the PMP is a great "minimum requirement." If you gave me a choice between 20 years of successful PM experience, and 3 years of experience with a PMP, guess which one I'm going to choose? But, everything else being equal, the PMP is valuable. If nothing else, having a standard jargon allows project managers to discuss issues without requiring translators. Isn't that valuable? It provides exposure to the basic concepts and at least shows you what you don't know. PMI and [the] PMP are not guarantees of success. By the way, I don't think that PMI makes any kinds of guarantees like that (hey, imagine the liability!)[3]

Demand for Additional Career Development Options

PMI reports that the number of project managers receiving its PMP certification has increased at an annual rate of around 20 percent for each of the past few years.[4] Jeff Moad, Executive Managing Editor for eWeek.com, notes that

125

"Median bonus pay levels received by PMP holders—15 percent as of the fourth quarter of last year—top the list of all certifications tracked by Foote Partners LLC, a New Canaan, Conn., compensation research company."[5]

With the numbers of project managers rapidly increasing in recent years, and with a large and growing body of PMPs asking "What's next?" there is a strong need for clear career development options beyond the knowledge-based PMP. Dr. Harold Kerzner, Executive Director of the International Institute for Learning, notes:

> In organizations that successfully manage their projects, project managers are considered professionals and have distinct job descriptions. Employees usually are allowed to climb one of two career ladders: the management ladder or the technical ladder. (They cannot, however, jump back and forth between the two.) This presents a problem to project managers, whose job responsibilities bridge the two ladders. To solve this problem, some organizations have created a third ladder, one that fills the gap between tech-nology and management. It is a project management ladder, with the same opportunities for advancement as the other two.[6]

If leading companies are starting to provide career paths for project managers, then there must be a corresponding development path to help the project managers acquire the skills they will need to succeed in each of the career development stages. In addition to obtaining these skills, project managers will need associated qualifications to demonstrate that they have achieved the required knowledge and skills. Max Wideman, PMI Fellow and past President, supports the need for additional qualifications to meet this demand:

> We would like to see some more globally accepted qualifications that reflect progressive levels of both learned knowledge and practical competence in the project management discipline.[7]

Career Development Options

This book helps project managers plan out their career development by providing background context and information on additional PM qualifications that a PM can use to build his or her career roadmap.

The first step in preparing a career development roadmap is to choose a standard benchmark against which you can compare yourself. There are many benchmarks for this comparison, some for project management knowledge, and some for project management competence. You may look at the IPMA's *International Competency Baseline* (discussed in Chapter 9), a national benchmark such as the Australian *National Competency Standards for Project Management* (see Chapter 10), PMI's *Project Management Experience and Knowledge Self-Assessment Manual*, or even a knowledge-based assessment such as the United Kingdom's *APM Body of Knowledge Self-Assessment Form*[8] (discussed in Chapter 9).

Next, you must have your knowledge and skills assessed against the benchmark. Usually, this is best handled through a self-assessment programme. Sue Beavil, Head of Professional Development for the Association for Project Management, notes that self assessment allows you to determine your weaknesses in a way that is open and non-threatening, though it does require honesty and objectivity to get meaningful results.[9]

Once you have been assessed, you can compare yourself against your chosen benchmark to determine possible development opportunities. You must be realistic, however – you cannot make up for all of your shortcomings at one time – select a small number (3 or 4) of areas that you would like to develop. Make sure that the areas are required for your present or anticipated jobs; look at the emerging trends in the marketplace.

Finally, once you've determined the areas you'd like to develop, you can start to plan out how you will improve on these areas. This is where an understanding of the two main types of qualifications is helpful: those qualifications that state that you have a requisite level of knowledge in the various areas of project management, and those that state that you are competent in applying your project management knowledge to successfully deliver projects. Chapter 2 discusses the distinction between knowledge and competence as it applies to project management.

Chapter 3 describes the Project Management Professional (PMP) qualification from the Project Management Institute – what it does test, and what it does not. Recent criticisms of the qualification are largely based upon misunderstanding the fundamental differences between knowledge-based and competency-based qualifications discussed in Chapter 2. Additional criticisms have been raised about the applicability of the PMP examination to the practice of project management in other countries around the world. As PMI pushes forward with its globalization agenda, project management practitioners need to understand better the debate and its implications; both sides have good points to consider.